LIFE IN
COLONIAL AMERICA
HISTORICAL COLORING BOOK

PETER F. COPELAND

DOVER PUBLICATIONS
GARDEN CITY, NEW YORK

For Andrew Mathieson

Life in Colonial America, Historical Coloring Book was originally published by Dover
Publications in 2002 as *Life in Colonial America Coloring Book*. The text was updated in 2023.

ISBN-13: 978-0-486-85226-3
ISBN-10: 0-486-85226-1

Manufactured in the United States of America
85226101   2023
www.doverpublications.com

Introduction

In 1492, Christopher Columbus sailed for Spain in an effort to discover trade routes to the Far East and India. This was the critical moment in the exploration of the Americas, as word of Columbus's voyages spread and other Europeans joined in the search for trade routes. Eventually, expeditions set out from Europe in order to colonize the New World, with Spain, Portugal, England (also called Britain), France, and the Netherlands taking an interest in the vast continent. From furs and fish to cedar logs and sassafras, the varied opportunities for trade and profit led to many expeditions.

Many settlers worked the land or joined the booming tobacco trade. The appeal of the new land was not limited to economic reasons. People escaped religious persecution or looked to worship as they pleased, including Quakers in Pennsylvania, Puritans in New England, and Catholics in Delaware.

Life was difficult for common people. Many arrived as bondsmen, indentured servants, and slaves. Relations between settlers and Native Americans were often hostile. Many colonists died from illnesses such as malaria and dysentery. Food was scarce, and adequate medical care was lacking.

This book depicts many aspects of life in colonial America before 1776: how the colonists lived, dressed, and traveled, along with some events that led to the creation of the United States. The book begins with the passage to and arrival in the Americas and concludes with the signing of the Declaration of Independence. Various colonists and adventurers are depicted, including the Dutch, English, Swedish, French, and Spanish. The book also addresses the treatment of Native Americans, who already inhabited North America, and African slaves, who were brought over to the New World.

A Passage to the New World (Early 1600s)

The 13 colonies that eventually became the United States lay along the Atlantic coast of North America. In the early seventeenth century, the English began arriving in wooden sailing ships such as the *Mayflower*. The ships were full with people seeking new lives in a new land. The hard journey from Europe to North America took several months.

Arrival in the New World (Early 1600s)

Jamestown, Virginia, founded in 1607, was the first successful English settlement in America. Other colonies were founded in Massachusetts, Connecticut, Rhode Island, Delaware, Maryland, Georgia, the Carolinas, and Florida. These *Mayflower* passengers are arriving on the rocky shores of New England.

Encountering Native Americans (Early 1600s)

Upon arriving in North America, Europeans were met by Native Americans. Many of the early colonists were not skilled at farming, hunting, or fishing. If not for the friendly Native Americans who taught them survival techniques, they would have starved to death before the crops they had been taught to plant could grow to maturity. These disembarking colonists catch sight of the Native American inhabitants.

Spanish Settlement at St. Augustine, Florida (Early 1600s)

In 1565, St. Augustine was the first settlement that the Spanish established north of Mexico. For many years, it was not much more than a military camp. It was one of a chain of forts built to protect Spanish shipping in the Caribbean Sea. St. Augustine survived as the oldest city in North America. These people are gathering in the plaza of colonial St. Augustine.

The Lost Colony

In search of a sea route to China, English explorers landed on the coast of Virginia in 1587, and they established a small colony. Three years later, a returning English expedition found the colony deserted. The only traces of the colonists were the letters "CRO" carved in a tree trunk and the name "CROATOAN" carved near the gate to the deserted colony. Among those missing was Virginia Dare, the first child born to English parents in the colonies.

Building Houses in Massachusetts Bay Colony (1627)

Nearly all of the colonists' homes in New England were built of rough logs cut into regularly shaped timber. The houses had thatched roofs like those seen in small English villages. Walls were constructed of woven branches plastered over with mud. These colonists are thatching a roof.

Clearing Land and Building Houses in the Maryland Colony (1634)

The Maryland Colony was established along the Potomac River, near the estuary with Chesapeake Bay, where the city of St. Mary's was built. The first houses were simple wooden cabins. Brick houses soon replaced them.

New Sweden (1638)

A colony of Swedes was established along the banks of the Delaware River. The colonists built Fort Christina near present-day Wilmington, Delaware. They set up the same type of log cabins that were built in Sweden. These simple houses, which could be constructed using no tools other than axes, were the prototype for the American frontier log cabin.

A Dutch Patroon and His Wife (ca. 1640)

The patroons were Dutch citizens who agreed to bring settlers to New Netherland in exchange for land. Many owned great estates in what is now upstate New York. The patroon is shown wearing breeches and a close-fitting jacket of rich velvet. His soft felt hat is decorated with ostrich plumes. His wife wears a red silk gown with cuffs and ruff of starched lace as well as an apron of fine Holland linen.

Puritans of the Massachusetts Bay Colony (1640)

The clothing worn by the Puritans of the Massachusetts Bay Colony was restrained, both in color and cut. The religious Elders controlled such matters, and everybody dressed according to what the Elders ordained to be decent. In the second half of the seventeenth century, the ordinances of the Elders carried less weight and fashions from London became popular. Children's clothes had the same patterns as their parents' attire.

A Colonial Bedroom

In the simple one-room houses built by the early colonists, the family slept in a bed built into one corner of the room. Children's beds were kept under the parents' bed, to be pulled out at night. The baby's cradle was set at a safe distance from the fire, although close enough to take advantage of its warmth.

A Colonial Kitchen

On a cold winter day, the kitchen was the warmest and most comfortable room in the colonial house. There might have been a venison stew bubbling in an iron pot in the large brick fireplace, along with a pair of rabbits browning slowly in the iron broiler below a hanging kettle. A musket and a powder horn, which carried gunpowder, might have been hung within easy reach above the fireplace.

A Colonial Shipyard (1650s)

Ships were in demand, especially for voyages to England and the West Indies. Every colonial seaport had at least one shipyard. American merchants shipped their cargoes on American-built ships. English shipowners were happy to buy American-built ships for much less than those built in Europe. In the years to come, American-built ships dominated oceans around the world.

Dutch New Amsterdam (1653)

The Dutch established a fur-trading station in Albany on the Hudson River in 1614, but it was not until 1623 that the first trading post was established on the island of Manhattan by the Dutch West India Company. The seaport of New Amsterdam, capital of the Dutch colony of New Netherland, is shown thriving.

A Post Windmill

The windmill was introduced by the Dutch in New Amsterdam. The "post" windmill headed its sails into the wind while rotating around a huge center post, balanced by a beam-mounted wheel that revolved as the mill turned. A second variety, the "smock" windmill, had a mushroom-shaped cap, which revolved with the changing winds.

Sir William Berkeley, Royal Governor of Virginia, and Lady Berkeley (1676)

Sir William Berkeley's harsh rule was addressed in a document drafted by the people of Virginia. Growing class distinctions, high taxes, and a perceived bias toward Native Americans had alienated his subjects. Nathaniel Bacon led an antigovernment movement, Bacon's Rebellion, demanding reform from Berkeley and the House of Burgesses, a legislative body. Several months later, Bacon and his men burned down Jamestown. The royal governor is dressed in red, with gold-laced buttonholes, buttons, and binding on his black hat. Lady Berkeley wears a pale blue dress trimmed in white with a white apron and sleeves.

An Ox Team (ca. 1680)

The ox was the original work animal in colonial America. Ox teams were used for all sorts of tasks, such as gathering hay, plowing, hauling rocks and tree stumps from cleared fields, and taking sap from sugar maples. Ox teams could still be seen on New England farms until well into the twentieth century.

A Hunting Party (ca. 1685)

Early colonial farmers supplemented their often meager diet by hunting the abundant wild animals in the fields and forests. This food source might have been all that stood between the early settlers and starvation. For later colonists, hunting became a sport. A group of hunters is seen out for an afternoon of sport.

An Early Pennsylvania Farm Home (1680s)

This mountain cabin, built of logs with the bark left on, could be quickly erected with a minimum of tools, as could the split rail fence. A stick-and-mud chimney was built outside and above the fireplace, which was constructed of rocks. The rifle-wielding farmer, wearing a homemade hunting shirt, is on his way to hunt game for the table, assisted by his dogs. The farmer's wife is boiling hog grease and lye to make soap for the family.

Native American Slaves in Charles Town, South Carolina

By 1685, the port of Charles Town, South Carolina, shipped deerskin to England and slaves from the Stono tribe to the West Indies. Rice became a leading crop for export. African slaves were soon imported from West Africa on slave ships. Many Native American slaves got sick in the malaria-infested rice fields and died.

On the Deck of a Slave Ship

The importation of slaves from West Africa was a large-scale business by the end of the seventeenth century. It continued in ever greater numbers until the slave trade was outlawed in the early nineteenth century. Slaves were bought and sold in all 13 colonies until the time of the American Revolution, when the slave trade was largely forbidden in the Northern colonies. African slaves were regularly forced to exercise, with crew members using whips.

The Deerfield Massacre (1704)

The town of Deerfield, Massachusetts, was raided by French soldiers and their Native American allies in 1675 and 1704, during France and England's colonial wars. Inhabitants of the village who were not slain were marched north to French territory in Canada. The village minister, the Reverend John Williams, was allowed to return to Massachusetts, where he wrote an account of the events. These members of the Abenaki tribe are attacking and burning houses during the 1704 massacre.

Colonial Dressmaking

The working dress of the poor was simple and well-made, typically constructed of coarse fabrics and homespun materials. The dress of the wealthy was often made of velvet and silk and edged with gold and silver lace. The clothing was almost always made to order. Few garments could be purchased ready-made, and they were mainly for slaves and poor workers such as sailors. This lady is being fitted for a gown by two seamstresses. Her dress is made of striped silk, with fine Holland linen sleeves.

Slaves in a Southern Plantation Kitchen

On Southern plantations, the kitchen was a building separate from the house. The wall contained a fireplace with a swinging iron crane, upon which pots and kettles could be hung over the fire. Corn was a staple of the diet; it provided food for the family and servants and was brewed into beer. Meat was preserved by salting and smoking it in a smokehouse, a small house behind the kitchen. Well-to-do people were hearty eaters, and colonial planters were no exception. These house slaves are preparing the evening meal.

A Horse Race

Horse racing had become a popular sport in the colonies in the early eighteenth century. In 1715, *The Boston News-Letter*—the first American newspaper to publish more than one issue—mentioned a horse race for a prize of 100 pounds. Other popular colonial sports were bowling and football, which was played in Massachusetts as early as 1686.

French *Voyageurs* in the Northwest Forest (1730s)

The French began exploring the North American interior as early as 1604 and soon took expensive furs home from Canada. Samuel de Champlain founded his first settlement on the St. Lawrence River in 1604 and began a brisk trade in beaver pelts, which were highly valued in Europe. Soon the *voyageurs* (travelers) of New France pushed westward in pursuit of the lucrative fur by trapping, trading, and forming alliances with Native American tribes, while exploring the Great Lakes and Hudson Bay as well as the Mississippi and Missouri rivers.

A Sailors' Tavern in Boston (1735)

In colonial days, the tavern provided food and lodging for travelers and horses. It also offered refreshment and amusement to neighbors. The tavern was a meeting place where news could be gathered. Taverns were the center of life, where even a royal governor might be seen and where drinking and having a good time were not forbidden. At a sailors' tavern in Boston, this young man is being directed into a life of adventure on a man-of-war (naval warship) or a privateer (armed pirate ship) during one of the colonial wars of the 1700s.

Bringing Tobacco to Market

Tobacco had been a profitable crop in Virginia and Maryland since the early days of those colonies. It was exported to European markets. Ships docked at large plantations. Other planters moved their crops there along a "rolling road," where slaves rolled huge barrels by hand or transported them with horses and oxen.

Reading the Newspaper (1740)

Newspapers began to be printed in Europe in the late seventeenth century and in America soon afterward. The colonial reader could get the "latest" news—which was weeks old—from England plus news from other colonies and accounts of laws passed in Parliament that related to colonial life and trade. The few newspapers that existed in the colonies were eagerly passed from hand to hand, especially in smaller towns and villages. America's first newspaper, the weekly *Boston News-Letter*, was launched in 1704. In the years leading up to American independence, the demand for news increased and the number of newspapers did too.

George Washington as a Young Surveyor

As a boy, George Washington learned surveying, which involved determining the borders of property. He carried out much of his work along the western frontiers of Virginia. Washington was the surveyor for Culpepper County, Virginia. The young Washington is shown surveying with Benjamin Banneker, an African American who became a respected mathematician, astronomer, and inventor. Trained as a city planner, Banneker was instrumental in designing Washington, DC.

Urban Crime in Philadelphia (1755)

Crimes committed by people in need were less common in the American colonies than in Europe. In the New World, a poor man—if he were free and white—did not suffer from the crushing poverty experienced by the lower classes in Europe. However, urban crime did exist. These two chimney sweeps are robbing and assaulting a gentleman on Lombard Street in Philadelphia.

The Funeral of General Braddock (1755)

During the French and Indian War, the colonists supplied colonial regiments that fought alongside the British against the French and their Native American allies for control of North America. General Edward Braddock, commander in chief of the British forces in North America, was killed in battle. Although highly skilled in military tactics, Braddock lacked knowledge of the wilderness. George Washington, the colonel of the Virginia regiment, led survivors back to safety. Washington is shown attending Braddock's funeral.

A Dutch Wagon (1750s)

Travel by land was limited because the roads were in bad shape and there were few bridges. Transport by water was preferred. Early land transport was carried out by horses and wagons, such as this Dutch wagon. The Dutch wagon hauled produce, supplies, and farm equipment, among other cargo.

Quebec (1759)

The British and French fought 5 colonial wars between 1689 and 1760 to determine who would control North America. The British conquest of Quebec in 1759 and the French surrender of Canada to the British in the Treaty of Paris in 1763 ended these conflicts. Britain and Spain became the major colonial powers on the continent, with Russia in control of Alaskan territory. British officers and a lady are shown walking and talking on the streets of conquered Quebec, with the damage from fire and British shelling noticeable in the background.

A Frontier Fort (1760s)

The first structure that the early colonists raised in the new land was a fort. Forts protected them from European rivals who might seek to take over the colony as well as Native Americans reacting to intrusions on their hunting land. Many forts became trading posts and meeting places for travelers. This fort is on the Virginia frontier.

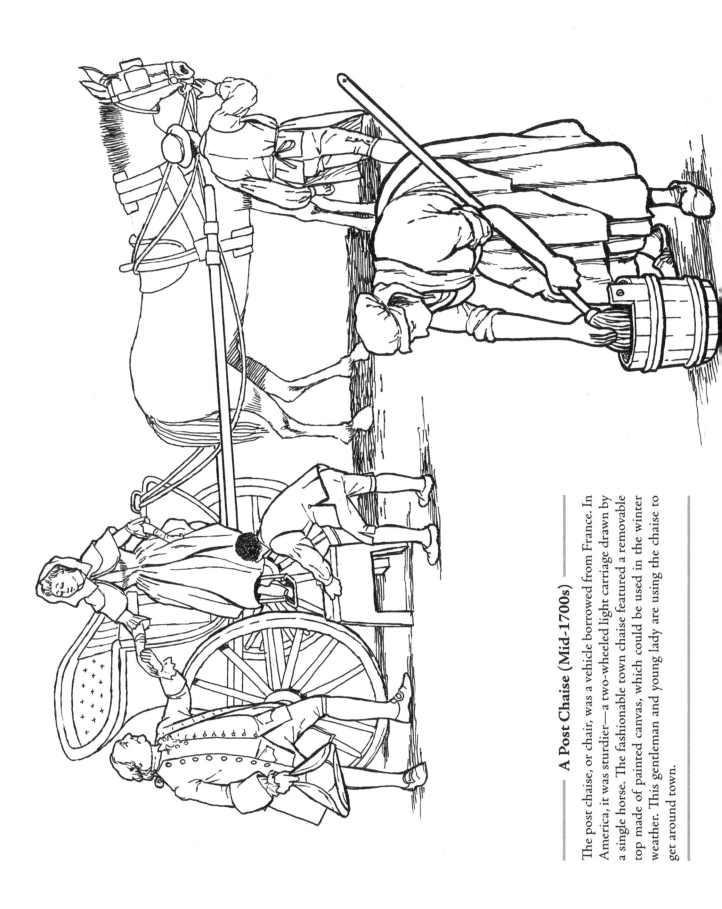

A Post Chaise (Mid-1700s)

The post chaise, or chair, was a vehicle borrowed from France. In America, it was sturdier—a two-wheeled light carriage drawn by a single horse. The fashionable town chaise featured a removable top made of painted canvas, which could be used in the winter weather. This gentleman and young lady are using the chaise to get around town.

A Native American Fort in the Appalachian Wilderness (1765)

In some remote mountain areas, where there were few settlers, there were Native American forts on hilltops, perhaps overlooking valley farms. The fort was a two-story log cabin with gaps between the logs so that rifles could fire through them. Native American forts were either permanent residences or only inhabited when warfare was expected. A few such buildings still stand in western North Carolina and southwestern Virginia.

A River Ferry (ca. 1770)

As the quality of roads improved, bridges were built across narrow streams. They were usually nothing more than logs across a stream from bank to bank, with boards or limbs laid across them. Flatboat ferries crossed rivers. Local landowners often added to their income by building and operating ferries, which were wide enough to accommodate a horse and wagon or a small number of cattle, horses, or oxen.

A Stage Wagon (ca. 1770)

The stage wagon had backless benches for passengers, and only a few riders got to sit in the rear, where they could lean against the frame of the wagon. Typically, nine passengers rode inside and a tenth sat in front with the driver. On both sides, leather curtains could be rolled up or let down. There was no heat or glass windows to protect passengers in the winter. The stage wagon was uncomfortable, and the later stagecoach was not much better.

A Spanish Priest in California (1771)

Although Spain had claimed California since the sixteenth century, it had done nothing there except allowing Catholic missions that targeted Native American inhabitants. In the 1760s, when Russia traveled down the western coast of North America, the Spanish established armed settlements between Los Angeles and San Diego. This priest at Mission San Antonio is accompanied by his basset hound, among local children.

Lamplighter (ca. 1775)

Only the biggest colonial cities had streetlights. Installation began in the years preceding the American Revolution. Philadelphia had streetlights installed and operating by 1762. In addition to lighting lamps in the evening and extinguishing them at dawn, the lamplighter cleaned lamps, trimmed wicks, and filled pans with oil. This lamplighter is filling the oil pan of a streetlight in Philadelphia.

Militia Muster (1775)

Each colony had a militia. Militia members practiced on the village green under the direction of officers, who were usually prominent citizens with military experience. The drills continued long after the colonies became states. These patriotic citizens are practicing a drill with muskets on the eve of the American Revolution.

Pulling Down a Statue of King George III (1776)

The relationship between Britain and the colonies grew more divided following the last of the wars with France. By 1775, fighting between British troops and American patriotic forces increased. Resentment and anger toward all things British led to the destruction of symbols of royal authority. This New York City mob is pulling down a statue of King George III.

The Declaration of Independence (1776)

After a year of warfare, colonist leaders approved the Declaration of Independence on July 4, 1776. This historic document announced to the world that the 13 former British colonies were independent of Britain and were self-governing, bringing about the end of the colonial American experience and the birth of the United States. The signers, from left to right, are Benjamin Franklin, Thomas Jefferson, John Adams, and John Dickinson.